Sh**ort report cartel**

HOW TO _PRINT_ Money FROM _SIMPLE_ Designs

By

Teslim Tiamiyu

You're Not Allowed to Sell or Share this report with anyone in any form! Be it printed or electronic.

If you try, I advise you to get your Advocates ready.

Make sure you choose the best ones though.

Because you're going to have a **very terrible legal experience**!

Legal Stuff:

I've tried to be as accurate as possible with the information provided in this report.

However, you're advised to use your native intelligence to make wise and accurate decisions.

Whatever outcome comes from the use or application of the information provided in this report is your own individual responsibility. The author doesn't assume any responsibility.

Additionally, this report isn't intended for use as legal financial or business advice, Services of appropriate consultants should be sought when needed.

Rebel Publishing Inc or Teslim Tiamiyu isn't a financial or business consultant.

Dear Friend,

Thanks for getting my report □.

I promise you'll get an equivalent value for your investment.

And if you can put the resources and bonuses I've attached with this report to good use.

You have a high chance of achieving Financial freedom in the next couple of months.

By the way, my report comes with a **Lifetime, NO Questions Asked Money Back Guarantee.**

Unless you get to learn one or two things from these reports or implement them all through, **don't hesitate to send me a sharp email via** hoyewummyteslim@gmail.com

Table Of Contents

Module One

<u>The Secret of a $179.5 Billion Business.</u>

$1,000 per second

$66,000 per minute

$ 4, million per hour

$100 million per day

$700m million per week

$37.4Billion per year

That's how much Nike makes from selling sports wares.

Many people who buy shoes or clothes from Nike are simply not aware of this.

But Nike doesn't **own** a shoe or clothing factory, they simply sell the Nike brand.

Using the same business model you are about to discover In this short report. Nike has built a ***$179.5 billion*** business.

What's A Print On Demand Business?

Print-on-demand is a simple business model that allows you to monetize simple graphic designs.

You simply have to come up with an interesting design, upload it and let a POD partner do the remaining work for you.

They handle your shipping, product creation and delivery, and every other headache that comes with running a business.

What Do You Need To Start A Print-On-Demand Business?

You need four things

1) A Business Mindset
2) A POD partner
3) An online store
4) Of course, You need designs (lovely ones □)

The remainder of this report will be discussing how you can get these four things in place.

Step One: Have A business Mindset

When people go into business. They do so for various reasons. To sort urgent bills, take care of their family, and enjoy the freedom that comes with entrepreneurial life. And a host of other reasons.

While these reasons might not be important at first. They form the foundation of everything. And decide whether a person succeeds in business or not.

Because your reason is your **WHY.**

Your WHY is very important, so take your time to clearly define it. Because it will be the only reason for you to keep going when the going gets tough.

Listen up. Entrepreneurship is a very rough road. Some days you'll fail and other times things will be smooth and near perfect. If you're the type who doesn't want to fail, I'm sorry, but this is probably not for you. You might want to consider taking a job and stacking up promotions.

But if you want to go into business. Prepare your mind and define your
WHY.

Pro tip☐:   *Make sure your why is strong enough.*

You must understand that this is business, the real world. And what matters
here is your ability to go all in and put in your utmost best.

Perhaps you didn't do well in school, and you think that certain things are
beyond you, or some achievements are meant for certain people. The"they".

But you are wrong! Nothing can be further from the truth. Nothing is beyond
you.
 What you need is a determination to succeed. The discipline to push yourself
beyond your limits.

I leave you with the following book recommendations to boost your mindset
and set your mind right.

- Think And Grow Rich By *Napoleon Hill*
- Rich Dad Poor Dad by *Robert Kiyosaki*
- No Excuses by *Brian Tracy*
- Atomic Habits (one of the best books I read during NYSC) by *James Clear*
- The Secret of Power Performance by *Roger Dawson*
- How To Turn Yourself into a Live Breathing Cash Machine By *Toyin Omotoso* (I've attached the first 24 pages as a bonus)
- Small Business Big Money by *Akin Alabi*

Action Step 2

<u>Choose A Suitable Niche</u>

The niche is all about the kind of products you want to be selling:
Various print-on-demand products include;

- Mug
- Shoes
- Towels
- T-shirts
- Pulse
- Handbags
- Wristwatch
- Handmade Bracelets
- Notebooks
- Phone Covers
- Stationary
- Sticker
- Hoods
- Posters
- Jackets and sweatshirt
- Pillows
- Bedsheets and blankets
- Yoga pants
- Leggings
- Wall art
- Kitchen accessories
- Kids' Clothing and Toys

Action Step 3

<u>**Create Your Designs**</u>

There are three ways to get stunning designs to use.

1. Create the design yourself
2. Hire Freelancers on Fiverr
3. Use AI tools to generate free designs
4. Get Ready-made designs.
5. Hire Good Graphic Designers

Whichever you choose, you need to know what designs are currently selling well. And an easy way to do this is via:

- DS Amazon Quick View or
- Prettymerch.com

Both of them are Chrome extensions and they only work on desktops.

But you can also type best-selling designs on Etsy on Google to see some really good designs.

How to Create Designs Yourself-

It is not a bad idea to create your designs yourself. But make sure you have an idea of the top designs that are already selling fast. That will give you a firm foundation of what to create.

Truth is, new designs sell fast, but you also need to understand that *new designs are a result of new ideas,* and the *new ideas are merely a combination of old existing ideas.*

If you want to learn how to come- up with new amazing ideas fast, I have added as a bonus, a very short report titled" **Techniques For Producing Ideas**". Pick it up and read it now.

Here are a few tools you can use to create designs for yourself.

Canva- canva has a pro version and a free version. But of course, the pro version has a lot of features compared to the free version.

You can get the provision for as little as <u>N2800 per month</u> although there are other design tools like CorelDRAW.

Canva is best especially if you're using your smartphone to design.

Always save your design as PNG files to maintain quality.

Hire Freelancers

You can also hire freelancers on Fiverr for between $5 and $30 based on your budget or the freelancer you hire.

But before you hire any freelancer, make sure

1. You pay attention to the review on each freelancer before hiring them to avoid any disappointments or stories that touch. Usually, freelancers with 5 or 4☐reviews are the best.
*   check their previous works too.
*   Ask them to send samples of their work.
*   Read feedback from past clients.

If you want to hire Freelancers fast on Fiverr, go through this link. **Best Fiverr Freelancers**
(I get a little commission for it).

You Can Also Use AI tools

You can also craft any design of your choice using any of these AI tet-image tools.

- Midjourney
- Tryleap
- Colormind.com
- Canva AI
- Designer.microsoft.com
- OpenAI.com

Most of these tools are adapted to desktops.
But if you are using Chrome on your mobile device, you can always switch to desktop mode.

- simply click the three bars on the top right corner
- look for **switch to desktop mode**
- Click **desktop mode**

Note: I've added a bonus file of over **50 prompts you can model to generate designs with AI.**

How to get Ready-Made Designs You Can Start Selling Right Away

Perhaps you're too busy to create designs on your own. And you don't have enough money to hire Freelancers on Fiverr.

Here's how to get stunning designs you can start selling immediately for as little as $1...

Visit Creative Fabrica
(I get a little commission and it doesn't affect your cost)

Other options include hiring a professional graphics designer for around **N3000** or **N5,000 (if you are in Nigeria)** depending on how that Graphics Designer charges.

Now I'm sure you might be thinking, how can I hire someone for that amount. Listen up! Don't let your scarcity mindset ruin your business for you., Don't just hire any random graphics designer because you're trying to save money. What is worth doing at all is all worth doing well. Find a really good Graphics Designer.

If you don't know any Graphics designers around, I recommend you send a message to Raaj Concept, he's one of the best graphics designers I've worked with. Click here to reach out to him (**Raaj Concept**)

Module summary:
Have a winning mindset and treat this as a business
There are five ways to create your design
Design yourself, hire Freelancers, buy ready-made designs, hire a professional Graphics Designer, or use AI tools.

Exercise:
Come up with at least 5 designs for your chosen niche.

Step 4

<u>Get Print On Demand Partners</u>

Now you must have come- up with a good design for your product.

NB: You can use the same design to sell any of these products. Be it shoes, bags, towels, etc.
Now it's time you look for a <u>print-on-demand</u> partner to work with.

Like I said you only need it to create the design and leave the remaining part of the production headache to a reliable print-on-demand partner. What they do is print your design on the product and deliver it to the customer.

Since they are going to be playing a huge party in this. This is why you should be super-careful when choosing a print-on-demand partner, they determine the failure or success of your business.

Here are some criteria for choosing a reliable POD partner:

1. **They must have quality products**:

Since you only do the design and these guys (POD partners) come up with the product for example the mug, shoes, towels, or even a wristwatch.

You need to be very careful because people will only keep buying your product if your product is of good quality. That is why I recommend that you order at least one or two samples before you start selling.

2. *They must be able to deliver fast.*

3. *Their shipping rates must be reasonably cheap.*

Your goal is to make profit from your business. If you can pocket at least 40% of your income then it's simply not worth it. So look for pod partners that can allow you the maximum profit possible.

You can choose to sell your designs locally or internationally. If you're selling locally (within Nigeria) you'll most probably work with Nigerian POD partners. There's a ton of them. But as at the time of writing(updating) this report, I've only reached out to two or three you can reach out to.

Nigerian POD partners:
1. **Printivo**
2. **Didi tees** (https://wa.link/ut98ih)
3. **Nukreationz.com** (+234 706 733 6097)

And if you're selling internationally, You'll need Foreign POD partners who can take your designs across the border.
4. **Printify**
5. **Printful**
6. **Amazon Merch on Demand**
7. Tpop
8. Jetprint
9. Teelaunch
10. Local POD partners
11. Spod

The only problem with these guys is usually payment issues and all. Let's see how to quickly sign up on **Printivo**.

Sign up With A POD partner

- Go to **Printify.com**, **printivo.com**, Printful.com, or **Amazon Merch** to sign up.
- Enter your details
- Upload your design to launch your first product.

Note: Most POD partners print and deliver products to customers within 2-7 business days (Mondays through Fridays-business days only).

Now let's quickly talk about how you can get a storefront for your POD business.

Step Five

Upload Your Designs In A Marketplace or Storefront

Marketplaces you can sell your products include:

Nigerian:
1. **Website**

2. **Selar.co**
3. **Printivo**
4. **Gumroad**
5. **Paystack**
6. **Whatsapp catalog**
7. **Flutterwave**

Simply upload your T-shirt to your storefront or website. Once you get orders, you simply/swiftly forward your order to your print on demand partners.

Foreign storefronts:

8. **Woocommerce**
9. **Ebay.**
10. **Woocommerce**
11. **Amazon**
12. **Ecwid**
13. **Etsy**
14. **Shopify**
15. **Bigcommerce**
16. **Wix Wix**
17. **Flutterwave etc**

Another popular storefront you can use is a storefront known as Etsy. With over 90 billion monthly visitors. Etsy also helps sellers advertise products and charge only after these products are sold.

But I don't recommend Etsy, as they don't allow direct payment to Nigerian banks. And the only reason I'm talking about it here in this report is because it's my responsibility to give you every useful information you need to have to start a Print-on-demand business.

To use Etsy, You'll be required to have a UK or US bank account or address and most importantly a UK or US mobile number, to process payments on **Etsy**.

Well, I did a little digging Which might be helpful.

You can download a virtual payment app like Grey to secure a US or UK bank account.

An efficient way to get paid fast is to have a foreign account.
If you would love to create a fast foreign account. Within a few minutes Click this link to do that with Grey: *https://greyapp.page.link/B4Um1FDTb9k9xh3k9*

And to get a Foreign phone number, you can download this app below. Numero. It's readily available on playstore.

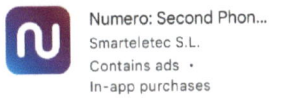

Numero: Second Phon...
Smarteletec S.L.
Contains ads · In-app purchases

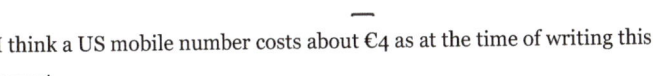

I think a US mobile number costs about €4 as at the time of writing this report.

But if you're NOT willing to go through the stress of getting a foreign account or getting a foreign mobile number, you can simply...

- Link your Printify with eBay, Shopify, and Woocommerce or;
- Link your Printful store with your **ECWID, eBay or Amazon seller accounts** store.

Whichever way you do it, it works.

Note: Woocommerce works hand-in-hand with WordPress websites. This means you'll need a proper website or domain name to use woocommerce.
But you can always get a website for as low as **N900/month at** domainking.com.
Simply Click on get hosting, each hosting comes with a free .com.ng domain name.

For the remaining part of this report, we will be focusing on using Printify and eBay for your POD business.

How to sign up on eBay

You can do this from your Printify account.

From your Printify account...
- Click on **my stores**
- Click on **add new stores**
- Click on **eBay eBay**
- If you don't yet have an eBay account, **create a new one**
fill in necessary details.

Also, upload the first product.

Enter all the details of the shop, the description of the product, and the shipping date.

Like I said, Printify delivers between 2-7 business days.

But to be on the safer side always put a back delivery date of about 2 days. From a little experience, people love companies or brands that under-promise and over-deliver more than those who over-promise but end up on that delivery. This shouldn't mean that you should not make good promises, just ensure that you are more than capable of your promises if you can deliver on the same day. It is smart to say you will deliver in 2 days.

And if you can deliver in 2 days or less it is smart to say you will deliver in 5 days.

People appreciate honesty and love brands that deliver their promises.

Note- 25 takes 60% of the total Revenue to cover the cost of the actual product printing and also delivery while you keep 40% as the brand designer.

Module summary:

In this module we have been able to cover

- **how to choose A POD partner for your business**
- **how to get a website for less than 900 naira/month**
- **how to sign up on Etsy as a marketplace**

next on the line we will be looking at in the various ways to sell your products on Etsy

Exercise for this module:

1. Create a printify account
2. Set-up your store on printify
3. Link your printify product with your Etsy store front
4. Get ready to sell

Step 6

Order Samples to Confirm Product Quality

Teslim
@Broken_copy

Any fool can make bulgous claims to get first time buyers.

But in the end, the one who delivers the most value keeps the customer.

REMEMBER, buyers are cheap. But Customers are rare.

First time buyers are easy to get BUT customers are as rare as *chicken teeth*.~Teslim (Yours truly)

Listen, No one really cares about how beautiful your website is or how big your company is.

I run my information marketing business from the corner of a room. And if you bought my *N2,000* report from me (actually that's the only way you'd be reading this right now), it simply means you felt a need to buy my product and have some of the information I have to share with you.

That's what really matters.

But the truth is, getting you to buy my first report is just the first step. If you'll ever buy another thing from me or my company (Rebel Publishing Inc.) you must truly love what you see inside this report.

That's the only reason you'll buy anything from me ever again.

And that's why I took out painstaking time to edit and re-edit all the information I put in this report.

So you can get the most value from it. And what time else, I made sure my report came with a Money-back guarantee, in case despite all my efforts, you still aren't really happy with me. You can always get your money back.

This is simply because a good reputation for delivering top-notch products will win you more opportunities than simply selling thousands of products.

So you want to make sure your product is of high quality. And that all your promises are duly delivered.

Because, no one really gives a damn whether your company is located in a rented room or not. What they care about is..

Can your product or service help them achieve their desires or solve their problems?

Can it truly deliver its promises?

Fix these two and you can keep customers for life.

And that's the essence of you first getting at least 2 or 3 samples of your designs before you start selling. That way you can have a feel of the product, their delivery and how fast they truly deliver to customers.

Creating a design or adding a product is just a first step. Anyone can do it. And sadly, that's exactly where most people stop.

And the result?

They end up shutting down their business or closing up that business and other times simply jump on another business.

But as my student, you are NOT allowed to do that, which is why I'm teaching you that..

Sales is the lifeblood of business.
You must get enough of it, if you're going to survive. Let's see how to get it.

Step 7

Selling Your Designs

A wise man Once said " Having a good product without Marketing it is like winking at a beautiful girl in the darkness of the night, you're winking, but the poor girl doesn't even know you're winking"

This quote has nothing to do with winking or seducing a girl.

But about selling.

Most people just create a product or have a business without marketing it. And simply expect potential customers to find them and also buy from them.

While this looks like a normal thing, the bad thing is that no matter how good your product is, if nobody knows that you have a product they want there is simply no way you'll be able to sell such a product.

And the only way to get people to know about your business or your product is to market such a product.

Which is why, for the remaining part of this report, we will be looking at the various strategies you can use to push your products on Etsy.

There are three main ways to push your Design :

1. SEO strategies (if you're selling on Marketplaces)
2. Running Marketplace ads (Amazon ads, eBay ads or Etsy ads)
3. Getting potential customers from social media (works best when selling from your Paystack,Selar, Flutterwave or Ecwid store)

Option No1

How To Get Buyers With Marketplace SEO Strategy
Your Store name

It all starts with your store name.

How you name your store affects your chances of selling well on etsy.
EBay has over 100 million shoppers or visitors coming to search for products to buy every single day.

A person looking for *bracelets* is likely to use keywords related to *'bracelets'* or something around *'fine bracelets'*. And someone looking to get shoes will probably check for *'amazing shoes'*, *'lovely shoes'*, *'new shoes'* or anything around this.

And if your store name doesn't include any of these highly searched keywords you probably won't be seen by shoppers And this decreases your chances of selling. For this reason, always follow lesson one which is :

Always include your niche in your store name.
You want to name your store Kezni? Don't call it *the Kezni store, instead* you should name it *Kezni bracelets*, this way people searching for *bracelets* will quickly locate your store as quickly as possible and probably buy.

Use captivating Images (and if possible videos):

We are in the world of Attention war.
And an average person has a lot of things distracting his mind;

A phone beeping in his hands;

a friend trying to talk to him about a hot gist;

A loud TV stirring him in the face with amazing pictures;

News outlets tempting him with the hottest updates of happenings around the world the past 24 hrs;

A blonde girl walking across the street in a bikini;

Notifications from Twitter, IG, YouTube, Facebook and all of that.

In short, you're competing with hundreds of these distractions for your potential buyer's attention.

Unless you manage to get hold of his attention fast within a few seconds, you will lose that potential buyer forever.

And when it comes to getting attention, NOTHING works better than "Incongruity"

Incongruity: simply means something unusual or out of place
Upload attention-grabbing images and videos that get your products in because wherever there is attention that's where the money goes.

Use captivating product descriptions:

Mirror your customers interest, Desire, and worldview.

Your description should also include accurate details of your product, the materials, the thickness etc.

Personalize Apple iPhone, Samsung Galaxy, and Google Pixel devices with premium-quality custom protective phone cases. Every case has double layers for extra durability and protection. The outer polycarbonate shell will resist daily impacts. Create a beautiful design, and we'll print it in picture-perfect quality with a glossy or matte finish.

.: Materials: 100% polycarbonate (shell), 100% TPU (lining)
.: Dual layer case for extra durability and protection
.: Available with a glossy or matte finish
.: Clear, open ports for connectivity
.: Blank product sourced from Korea

An example of product description.

Note: I've added a short Copywriting course "kick-ass Copywriting to teach you how to use words that bring in customers & also get attention. Make sure you go through it.

Option No2:

Running Marketplace Ads (eBay as a case study)

Promoted Listings are ads or sponsored items that allow sellers to increase their product visibility and sales. They're displayed in top places on eBay and may also appear in search results. eBay will pull the seller's promoted listing based on its relevance to the search and the going ad rate.

How eBay adverts work

eBay Promoted Listings is a pretty simple advertising scheme. You just choose which items to promote, and how much of the sale price you are willing to pay. eBay then boosts your items from their normal positions in the search results to the four top spots, or a variety of placements lower down in the results.

How to advertise to sell on eBay

You can promote your listings (products listed) using the Advertising dashboard,

- your listing tool,
- My eBay Active or Seller Hub Active listings.
- Select Create new campaign.
- Choose either Simple listing selection, Bulk listing selection, or Creating rules (automated campaigns)

With this, you can put your advert at the forefront of eBay Listings. When eBay visitors enter their site, you'll have a high chance of selling to them first. As your products will be among the top products depending of course on...

- How well the product is generally selling
- How high the search committee volume for the product is
- How much you put into the campaign. Amidst others

Getting Buyers From Social Media (Facebook)

There are a lot of social media platforms; Facebook, WhatsApp, Instagram, YouTube, tik-tok etc.

But there are only two ways to get potential buyers from any of these social media:

- **organic traffic** and
- **paid traffic**.

By organic traffic it basically means- to attract the right people by creating content they love will most likely relate with.

for example: If I want to build an audience of people who are interested in sales and marketing.

I'll start by talking about sales persuasion and anything that teaches how to get more sales Because that's what my ideal audience is most likely going to be interested in..

And if I plan on attracting people who are interested in fashion I simply have to start separating content around the latest fashion trends, the top trending celebrity designs and basically all to be in vogue.

Recently a friend of mine, Enny, wants to build a Pet brand on Instagram and I'll be helping him with this brand.

The only issue about organic traffic is that

- it takes a lot of time before you get results and
- it requires a lot of effort to come up with content and also create them and get in by your desired audience.

The second way to get potential buyers is via **paid adverts**.

And this is what the rest of this report is going to be all about.

How to get potential buyers from Facebook adverts

- **Create a Facebook profile**
- **create a Facebook page**
- **create a Facebook business account**
- **run your tummy hurts and**
- **target the right audience**

To create a Facebook personal profile all you need to do is..

- Go to facebook.com
- Enter your email address and phone number.
- Fill the necessary details
- And Ooops you have a Facebook profile.

To create a Facebook page:

- click the three bar on the top right side of the page
- next click on Pages
- then click on create
- click on get started enter favorite page and continue from there.

To create a Facebook business account

- go to business facebook.com
- create a business account business
- Enter business emails
- country and choose your type of business.

Note:

make sure you have a valid identification or any relevant ID cards in hand whenever you are opening a Facebook business account.

The reason is that recently Facebook Bans every newly-opened business account so unless you confirm your identity with a valid id card, there's simply no way you can use Facebook for business.

link your Facebook ad account with a website. don't worry if you don't have a website. **You can simply link your store to your social media page. It also works**.

Funding Your Facebook Ad Account

There are two options to fund your Facebook ad account. You can fund it with

1. **Direct Debit Card:** This can be any of your MasterCard or Visa cards.

2. **Payuu**.

Advise you to use Payuu, because it prevents the Facebook algorithm from storing your details. In case your other account gets banned you can always use the same debit card over and over again.

That way you can avoid sleepless nights that come with using Nigeria banks and a change in CBN policy by another EMEFIELE.
I had a very terrible experience in 2022 to 2023 trying to find my other account and I lost at least two Facebook accounts simply because I couldn't pay with my debit card. You don't want things like this.

Using **PAYUU** to fund your ad account. Make sure you don't fund it with too much money at the start.

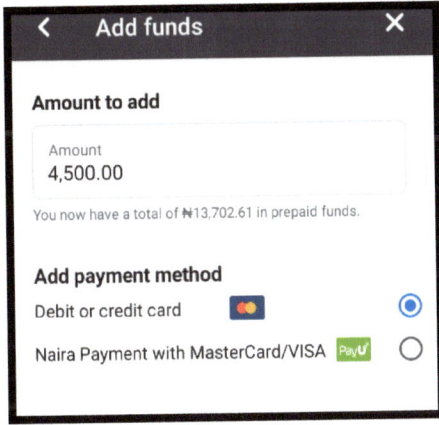

In fact I advise you to fund it with N500 at first. just to run a test advert. To warm-up your ad account and build trust with the Facebook algorithm.

A warm-up advert can be a post with useful tips like

- 7 top trending designs in 2023
- Tips for living a healthier life
- 6-most lucrative Business in 2023

I advise you to make your first advert a ***page like or post engagement campaign*** advert.

Because if you have reasonable number of **likes** on your page , you will be able to increase the credibility of the page and encourage the algorithm to trust you more. Once you run your warm-up advert it's time to run proper ads to get buyers to your store.

How to craft a simple Facebook ad creatives

I learnt this framework from a guy called Frank Kern.

Frank Kern is a mega successful entrepreneur and has created numerous successful Facebook ads campaigns that has brought in millions of Dollars for himself and his partners. He is often referred to by many expert marketers as the father of Facebook advertising.

Well, according to Frank kern, the secret behind his monstrous success is this: he keeps his ads stupendiously simple.

Here are three simple frameworks he taught people to use to write Facebook advert.

The first framework is what I call the I- A-H-H-H frame-work

If you're/ Are you.....

And you want...

Here's what...

Here's what to do...

Here's what to do next....

Examples;

Are looking for a simple way to start a profitable Online Business that brings in consistent income weekly *And you want* to do it without entering people's DMs, running adverts or asking people to buy anything from you. *Here's (what)* a simple way to earn in dollars right from your Smartphone in the corner of your room by simply uploading simple easy to create designs,(*Here's what to do*) simply copy my step by step guy and you can model the techniques to get started fast. (*Here's what to do next*) Simply Click the link below to get a free copy of my report.

second framework is what I call the CPEO framework

C stands for-Call them out e.g Are you a sit-at-home mom, if you're looking for a simple and affordable to look good

P- Problem or Desire- here's where you talk about their problem

E- Educate- teach them something new

O- offer- lay down your offer.

By the way, there are 3 things that a successful advert must do.

- Grab attention
- Hold attention
- Make an offer

If any of these is missing, there's simply no way your advert is ever going to convert.

Indicator Framework

Address their deep concern
Enter the conversation already going on in their head
Answer their burning questions
Make your offer.

Finally, the last technique I'm going to be sharing with you is what I call the **Whistle Blower Technique** I learnt from Mr Toyin Omotoso, the founder of Expertnaire.
it says to call out your audience.

Here's the psychology behind it,

Let's say you want to get a friend's attention or a friend of yours in a very crowded

if you want to call them from afar and get their attention,

Merely saying **hey you** will attract a lot of people in the same place .

so it's smart to say **hey Jide**, if your friend's name is **Jide**.

He's probably going to turn around and look back to check who's calling him.

And also since there are a lot of people who might be bearing **Jide**, it's even much stronger to call him by his full name "**Jide Animasaun**" or a childhood nickname that's very peculiar to him.

The lesson here is that, a powerful way to get anybody's attention is to simply **call out to them** by some of their characteristics like name, desires etc.

Take for example, this ad I wrote,

*The headline reads how a **sit-at-home** Dad built a 500k/month Business.*

As you can see, the keyword there is sit-at-home Dad.

And if you're writing an ad that addresses fat people:

How I lost 30kg of weight eating a little known Nigerian food.

.

If you are selling to Nigerians.
Your ads will be more effective if you have a live product in your hands and then create a video with it. Than to simply Post random faceless pictures displaying the product.

I honestly don't know why, but results have shown that such adverts convert better. Perhaps it communicates that your advert is real and that you're a real person. And Nigerians that I know love to deal with real and totally genuine people.

How to Target the right Audience on Facebook

Go to your Facebook Business manager,

Click on "***Ads Manager***"

Click on "***Audience***"

Create a saved audience

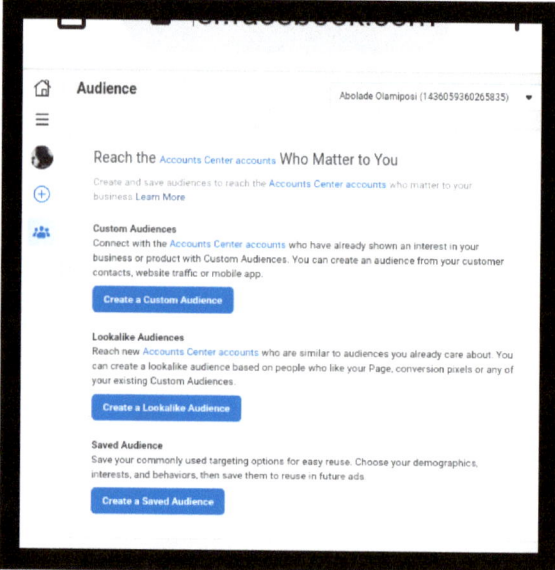

The kind of audience you're going to target depends on what kind of product you're selling.

And it's always good to have a clear understanding of who your ideal buyers are before you even think of running adverts.

If you're selling fashion products, you want to target People who are already buying stuff online.

Actually, there are three ways to target buyers on Facebook:

1. Behavior

2. Interest

3. Demographics

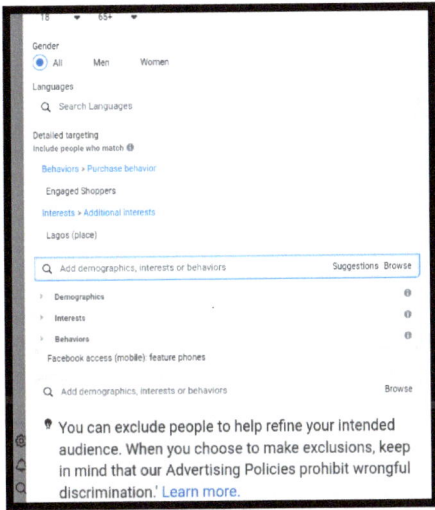

By behavior, I'm talking about their shopping behavior, are they the kind of people who buy things online or they've never bought before.

To target People who are already buying Online, include "***engaged shoppers***"

And with interest: this is talking about the topics they're interested in or simply passionate about.

For a product targeting women, I know a lot of women will be interested in *Nollywood movies, BBNaija* and stuff like that.

Whatever your audience is, you simply have to include these interests in your targeting.

And by Demographics, the location where your ideal buyers are living or using Facebook from.

You can decide to target People in Ilorin alone, or people in Lagos etc.

Note: Always exclude People with " feature mobile phones" from your ad.

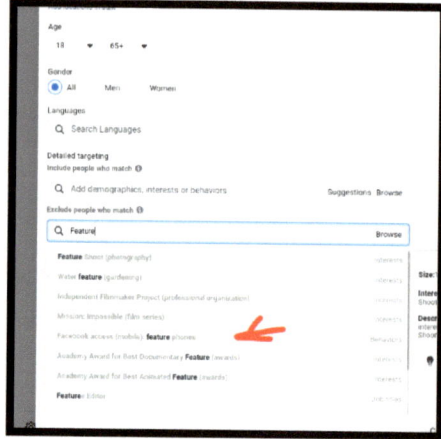

Because these are usually people who don't have any money to spend. You want to keep them away from your ad. You can also select some other devices that you want to include or exclude..

Alright, Now please understand that this isn't a complete guide on FB Advertising or targeting, it's just enough to help you in your POD Business.

If you want to learn more about Facebook Advertising (and I strongly recommend that you learn more), I strongly recommend   Emannuel Adiotu's Facebook ads made easy course

He used Facebook Ads to pull almost 10 million naira from a toothpaste Product in 2020, he's also the In-house ad expert for Africa's No.1 Digital

Marketing platform. The course sells for just 35,000 Which is really cheap compared to other FB ad courses I've seen. Check it here (*Facebook Ads Made Easy Course*)

Well, if you can't afford to buy a course on Facebook ad right now, it's fine. What's inside this report should be enough to put you through. But if you can, don't hesitate to get the course ASAP.

Now, please understand that not everyone that not everyone that clicks through your ad or adds your product to cart will buy immediately. All you have to do is simply follow up.

I think eBay automatically follows up on cart leavers. That might not be a serious concern if you're using eBay. But if you're using another storefront like woocommerce. You might want to create a follow-up sequence of about 5 emails for cart-leavers.

Summarizing the Process

<u>Step 1- Choose A Niche to focus on</u>
<u>Step 2- Create Designs</u>
<u>Step 3-Choose A POD partner to work with</u>
<u>Step 4- Choose A Storefront for your Design</u>
<u>Step 5- Order Samples</u>
<u>Step 6- Get Buyers/Collect Orders</u>
<u>Step 7- Send orders to your POD Partners</u>

Here we are, right at the end of this amazing report. Now you have all the four things you need to start a POD business. And you have a clear understanding of what a POD business is.

With this report and other resources I have put at your disposal, I hope you commit to implementing all through.

Cheers to your success.

PS- Have you got any questions you need quick answers to? Send me a quick email at <u>hoyewummyteslim@gmail.com</u> or you can forward your questions to the telegram support group.

Teslim Tiamiyu
Rebel Publishing Inc

Helpful Resources:

- **How A Graphics Designer Made Multiple Dollars on Etsy**
  https://youtu.be/if7PC150DBw
- **How to run my Multiple successful stores by Christopher States:** *https://youtu.be/yMkNHXy4eAI*
- **Etsy Tips And Secrets~ Paul Brown:**
  https://youtu.be/yMkNHXy4eAI
- **Zero to 1M by Olivier Jones: How he made £1 million selling Prints.** *https://oliverjones.gumroad.com/l/Rights*
- ***Courage Ngele:*** *How to make at least 500k from local Print On demand Business in 2023: https://youtu.be/RSywop_QyIQ*
- **Greg Gottfried: Full Print On Demand Tutorial for Beginners***: https://youtu.be/oWh4PP68RsE*

www.ingramcontent.com/pod-product-compliance
Lightning Source LLC
Chambersburg PA
CBHW040759240526
45474CB00008B/115